I HAVE NO WORDS

Cristina Volpe

BookLeaf Publishing

India | USA | UK

Presentation by *BookLeaf Publishing*

Web: www.bookleafpub.com

E-mail: info@bookleafpub.com

ISBN : 9789358362244

First edition 2021

*I would like to dedicate this booklet to my girls -
my love, my power, my joy. Let it out, be free,
follow your passion, dive deep.*

ACKNOWLEDGEMENT

Thank you M for encouraging me to complete this challenge. It has been so rewarding and energizing.

Feelings on Paper

Put your feelings down on paper.

But I have no words.

There is nothing. Like a day-three bag of chocolate chip cookies. I am bare, depleted, vacuous. Nothing left but crumbs, the memories of cookies ingested long hours ago.

At 2:30am and even at 4:00am I am a poet grandmaster.

Words like harsh, condemn, thrash, anamorphic.

I am lyrical and symphonic, a villain, the enfant terrible, inspiring.

Moved to murder the moon as it rests outside my despised window.

The shards of light that trespass into my room inflame me, provoke me.

Oh, the cruelty and stupidity.

Oh, the low-lifes and frauds.

Oh, the excess and depravity.

Oh, the starvation and makeshift sidewalk homes.

Oh, the slander and distortions.

Oh, the bricks of gold piling up and the penniless.

Oh, the grey and bland.

By the time the alarm chimes at 6:30am the fire has been stomped out, like a rhinoceros chasing the flame.

The hush of a new sun calms, mollifies, subdues my soul.

I am diminished. Reduced to kindness and a void.

The sleeky, anemic, insipid obligation to be nice, like morphine for the soul..

No hatred.

No screaming.

No ecstasy.

No tearing out of hair.

Yes, Sir. No, Sir. Of course, Sir. Please
and Thank You.

A roller coaster ride in super
slow-motion with the valleys stretched
and evened out.

I live my existence as a good girl,
mother, daughter, friend, worker.

Kind.

Hospitable.

Diligent.

Obliging.

Doting.

Dutiful.

I spill glitter as I amble, as if in a Gustav
Klimt painting.

Perhaps I am content.

I do not know.

You asked me to write down my feelings
but I do not know their name.

Longing.

My olive tree arrived in the mail.

"A part of Italy in your home."

Is what the label read.

I sat down on the floor and listened.

From far across the wide ocean

Came the murmur of the language,
voices, sounds.

The gondolier raised his leg to the wall
and pushed us further along the canal.

Later we moved slowly under the Bridge
of Sighs. Il Ponte dei Sospiri.

Grazie, Thank you.

Andiamo. Let's go.

A domani. See you next time.

It was true.

A part of Italy in my home.

White Walls

Bare walls surround me.

The perfect shade. Cool and crisp, a
northern landscape.

In the quiet minutes, in between
podcasts and phone calls, business
meetings and the whirling of machines

I lift my eyes to stare directly into the
empty vast white.

"I'm sorry. I cannot make up my mind."

The hammer and nails rest.

Facing the walls, one after another,
paintings, prints, quotes, mementos,
colours, words, black and white.

But if I dare to turn them around and use
my hammer and nail

Who will I become? Me? The real me?
Another version of me? Someone else's
version of me?

I am running out of time. I am moving
further and further away from me.

Bare white walls surround me.

In the quiet moments I feel their pulse. A
slow beat of panic and resignation.

Would he?

The car turned left.

He did not see her traipsing along, carefree and joyful, anticipating the sweetness of milk and cookies.

Smashed and cracked and crumpled and unaware.

The driver said she should have been more careful.

Would he have felt the same way if he saw her?

Bruised and battered? Screaming and laying still? Broken and stitched up?

Would he maintain his superiority in the face of her pain?

Does he have the same nightmares her sister does?

Does he ever wonder what became of the young child he hit?

Does he ever feel remorse?

Does he still drive his fast car?

Does he still drive his car fast?

I see her traipsing along, carefree and joyful, anticipating the sweetness of milk and cookies.

Hands

the moment

he touched me

a light touch

on the back of my hand

my blood quickened

holding my breath

until I turned

to look at him

eyes soft

searching

imploring me

not to run

but to touch his hand

again

There Was A Young Lady

There was a young lady from Truro.

Who said "There's no place I wouldn't
go."

So, she packed up her suitcase

Bikini and blanket, just in case.

And sailed cross the sea to Rialto.

Mementos

Each day I walk through Pimento

And I leave with a memento.

As I hold tight to the leaf

I am filled with such grief

For the tree that lost its child.

The Cool Down

I put the ice cubes in the bucket

And waited for them to melt.

Then I jumped in the bucket

To cool down.

May

Green

Rain

Warmth

Birthday

Rebirth

Emerald

Long days

Transition

Love

Death

The Shadows

When the walls creep forward

And the air thins out

Every word feels awkward

And full of doubt.

As the eastern sky darkens

And shame settles in

I crawl into the margins

To escape the din.

The Bottle

I prayed that he wouldn't come home.

This was my hope

As I tried to cope

The bottle was his best friend

But it was a dead-end.

Always one more

Always ready to pour

Running up to my room before he
opened the door

A confluence

of hate

and fear

and love.

But I was not able

to sit at the table

cause this was no fable.

It was life

It was strife

It was time to go.

Working From Home

Working from home

A balcony for an office

Above the din of the courtyard.

The sharp aroma rising out of the lilac
bushes.

The swing sways, as if remembering

The squeals of the freckled girl

Working the swing solo for the first time.

Picnic blankets laid down and watchful

Mothers eyeing the playground.

Sirens piercing the jubilation

Racing up and down the busy
boulevard.

I close my eyes

And wait

For the laughter to start again.

Away

Walking along the boardwalk

As the rain fell down

I slowly melted away.

The Meditation

I watch her on her balcony.

Huddled in the far corner.

Performing her nightly meditation.

Deep breath in.

Skunk breath out.

The Misanthrope

I missed you so much, he said.

A skilled architect

Crafting a false impression.

Concealing the anger under the
amenable facade.

Watching me from the street

Piling the lies, up, up, up.

So I stood in the rainstorm and washed
his essence away.

I watched as he tumbled forwards

His very being rushing down through the
sewer grate.

And then I blinked.

And in that moment

The flowers bloomed

The trees burst with tiny leaves

The grass turned green

The sky was blue

And I could smell lemon tea and almond
cookies.

What If?

If I had a boat

I would set it afloat

And sail to the open sea.

If I had a bike

And I don't mean a trike

I would ride to the end of the street.

If I had an airplane

One that had a weather vane

I would soar above the clouds to watch
the sunset.

If I had a pair of runners

Pink, red, stunners

I would run from city to city to city.

If I had a train

Click-clackety over the plains

I would feel at home under the
never-ending sky.

Hello Snowflakes

The weatherman said snow is coming.

And so I wait with bubbling delight.

A cup of hot tea between my hands.

Looking out the window

At the first snowflakes of the year.

Hello Snowflakes.

Welcome home.

The Mother and Child

From my seat

I watch.

And listen.

North of 33rd street she hops on.

I see her belly grow.

Her fashion evolves into clothes for two.

She is tired and bothered by the smells.

Of bodies unbathed

And spiced foods.

Then the bump is gone.

And a baby appears.

Held close.

Mother and child as one.

Wrapped in linen fabrics of orange and
grey and green and pink and white.

Soon the child walks.

And laughs.

And talks.

And argues.

And grows and grows and grows.

And one day she is traveling alone.

She says to the lady beside her.

Mom has gone to live with the angels.

Happiness

Does it exist?

Can it exist?

Not the sensation when you get an A+
or blow a big bubble

Or land the promotion or buy a house

Or slip the ring on the finger or smell
that newborn baby smell

But happiness with yourself.

Are you the person you wanted to be?

Are you the person you could be?

Are you you?

House Number Twenty

It was July driving north to the country.

Hoping to rest and let my mind wander free.

I packed the condiments

And all the other bits.

Then headed straight to house number twenty.

Before unpacking I headed down to the dock.

To listen to the natural world talk.

Mrs. and Mr. Loon.

Singing a celestial tune.

As the woodpecker tapped out the time like a clock.

Oh how I've missed that old wiry
mattress.

That by summer's end will have my
back in a tangled mess.

But the window faces west.

And the time I love best

Is watching the sun sink serenely into
the abyss.

I spend my hours putting words down on
paper.

Prose that I will never finish later.

I languish in the sun

With drinks and sticky buns

And long walks and quick dips in the
cold water.

When I arrive back in the city I am
disjointed.

This speed of movement is not what I
wanted.

But it pulls me in

And I become part of the din.

Til house twenty again leaves me
anointed.

Oh My

Oh my

What have I done?

I've looked him in the eye

And smiled.

Is he walking towards me?

No

He is walking away forever.